THE LIFE OF ST. MARY OF EGYPT

St. Sophronius,
Bishop of Jerusalem

Translated by: D.P. Curtin

Dalcassian Publishing Company
PHILADELPHIA, PA

THE LIFE OF ST. MARY OF EGYPT

Copyright @ 2019 Dalcassian Publishing Company

All rights reserved. No part of this publication may be reproduced, distributed, or transmitted in any form or by any means, including photocopying, recording, or other electronic or mechanical methods, without the prior written permission of the publisher, except in the case of brief quotations embodied in critical reviews and certain other non-commercial uses permitted by copyright law. For permission request, write to Dalcassian Publishing Company at dalcassianpublishing at gmail.com

ISBN: 978-1-0879-8041-6 (Paperback)

Library of Congress Control Number:
Author: Curtin, D.P. (1985-)

Printed by Ingram Content Group, 1 Ingram Blvd, La Vergne, Tennessee

First printing edition 2019.

THE LIFE OF ST. MARY OF EGYPT

THE LIFE OF ST. MARY OF EGYPT

LATIN TRANSLATOR'S PREFACE:

To the most glorious and distinguished lord Charles.

Knowing that your most glorious majesty is greatly pleased both with the divine utterances and the examples of the preceding saints, when long ago I presented to my lord the document of the conversion of Mary of Egypt, together with the scroll of the penance of a certain viceroy, because he himself had perished by some accident, now in the meantime I have devotedly obeyed your command in restoring the same. It was also my respect and devotion to present not only the simple text of the matter mentioned, but also to add other things worthy of inquiry, namely, concerning the venerable decrees and deeds of the prefect of the Roman Church: whose sanctions your majesty knows very well how reverently the Church uses them. Your servant has therefore taken this summary of brevity, so that your serenity, which I observe is greatly burdened with the burdens of the Republic, and which does not have time to go through the sparsely different volumes of writings, may hold certain ecclesiastical customs in brief, as if included in a certain Enchiridium, and because according to the interest of the royal industry I have learned, my lord, to be diligent in this, to direct your deeds and dictations according to your irrefutable authority, and what is to be held towards the divine worship, and what is to be rejected, diligently to search and scrutinize, to be of constant elucidation, how, protected by the help of his divinity, you may deserve to run in all things with successful success.

The author's prologue.

It is good to conceal the king's secret; but to reveal and confess the works of God is honorable (Tob. 12). For thus it is read, that the angel said to Tobias, after the loss of his eyes, and a glorious illumination, and after having passed through the dangers from which he was delivered, he obtained the mercy of God. Indeed, to reveal the king's secret is harmful and very dangerous; and to be silent about God's glorious works is a great loss to the soul. For this reason I, doubting to cover with divine silence, and fearing the impending judgment of the condemnation of the lazy servant, who took the talent from his master, dug it in the ground, and hid it in the earth, and gave it to work, hid it outside the business (Matt. 25), I will not be silent about the sacred narrative brought to me. But let no one be incredulous of me who writes about what I have heard, and let no one esteem me a liar, doubting the greatness of the matter. For it is far from me to lie about sacred things, and to adulterate the word where God is mentioned. But he, who understands little things, and is more unworthy of the greatness of God, who has assumed flesh, and is unbelieving of those who say these things, will not be a danger to me. But if those are those who read the text of this scripture, and refuse to believe the glorious wonder of the matter, and may the Lord have mercy on them, and make them capable of the holy word, lest there should be the miracles of God, which he predestined to be done more in his elect: since they themselves considering the weakness of human nature, they judge impossible things which are said of holy men to be glorious. Let me take up the narrative of the rest, relating the very thing, which is acknowledged to have been done in our generation, which a holy man, divine and brought up to act and teach, narrated. But as was said above, let no one draw these things to incredulity, considering that it is impossible for such a great miracle to happen in this generation of ours, because the grace of God passing through all generations into holy souls, makes friends of God and prophets, just as Solomon taught according to God (Song 7). For it is time to reveal the beginning of the sacred narrative, the great and manly struggle of the venerable Mary of Egypt, namely, how she fulfilled the times of her life.

LIFE

CHAPTER ONE.--In the monastery of Palestine there was a man adorned in manners of life and speech, who was carefully instructed in monastic acts from the very cradles, and brought up truthfully in manners, named Zosimas. And no one will esteem us to say that Zosimas was accused of another sect in preaching erroneous dogmas; for there is one here, and another that, and there is a great distance between them both, although each has been allotted one name of the term. Here, therefore, Zosimas from the beginning was converted in one of the monasteries of Palestine, and passing through all the monastic discipline, he became the most approved of all in the work of abstinence. For every precept handed down to him by the canons from those who had been brought up from childhood, he irreproachably preserved the struggle of a perfect monastic discipline. He also added many things to himself, desiring to subdue the flesh to the spirit. Nor is it proven that he has offended in anything. For he was so perfect in all monastic acts, that many a time many monks from the monasteries of the aforesaid place and from distant parts converging to him, bound themselves by his examples and doctrines, and subjugated themselves much more to the imitation of his abstinence.

CHAPTER 2.--Having all these things in him, he never departed from the meditation of the sacred speech, but resting on his bed, or rising, or holding work in his hands, or food, if it was convenient for him to take, he used spiritually the good which he was accustomed to use, he had one unbroken and never failing task, to chant frequently and meditate on the sacred speech. For many times they have asserted that visions have been shown to them by God, and this is not surprising nor incredible. For if, as the Lord says, blessed are the pure in heart, because they themselves shall see God (Matt. 5); how much more those who have purified their flesh, always sober, and vigilant in spirit, look forward to divine enlightenment, receiving the vision of the indication of the future goodness prepared from here? And Zosimas himself said that he had been handed over to this monastery by them, so to speak, with his mother's arms, and that he had completed a monastic course there until his fifty-third year. After this, he was struck by certain thoughts, as if he were already perfect in everything, not needing anyone else's teaching in anything. And this, as he said, he thought to himself: Is there a monk in the world who can give me something new, able to help me in something that I do not know, or that I have not accomplished in monastic work? Can there be found among those who led the desert a man who precedes me in deeds? While he was thinking these similar things, a certain one stood by and said to him: "O Zosima, well indeed, and as it was possible for a man, you have decreed, you have well completed the monastic course. However, there is no one among men who shows himself to be perfect. For the present struggle is greater than the past, although you do not know it. But that you may know how great are the other ways of salvation, go forth from the land and from your kinship and from your father's house, like Abraham, that great of the patriarchs (Gen. 12), and come to the monastery that is near the river Jordan."

CHAPTER 3.--Soon following the speaker, he left the monastery in which he had lived since his childhood, and arriving at the Jordan, the holiest river of all, he was directed by him who had called him to the monastery to which God had commanded him to come. Knocking at the door of the monastery, he first spoke to the monk who was watching the door, and he told him to the abbot. He who received him, and seeing his religious habit and appearance, after he had bowed his knee, as is the custom of monks, having received prayer, asked him this: Whence, brother, have you come? and why did you associate yourself with lowly monks? But Zosimas answered: "When indeed I came, I do not think it necessary to say; but the grace of building, Father, I have come. I have heard of you great things and worthy of praise, and of being able to associate the soul with God." And the abbot said to him: "God, brother, who alone heals the infirmity of the soul, may he himself teach you and us the divine commandments, and direct all to do those things which are expedient. For man is not able to edify man, unless each one attends to himself frequently, and works with a sober understanding of what is expedient, having God as his co-worker. However, since, as you said, the charity of Christ has led us humble monks to see you, stay with us, if for this reason you have come, that the good shepherd may nourish us all by the grace of his Holy Spirit, who gave his life as a ransom for us and calls his own sheep by name (Matt. 20; John 10)." When the abbot had said these things, bending his knees again, Zosimas received the prayer, answered Amen, and remained in the same monastery.

CHAPTER 4.--And there he saw the elders shining in their actions and vision, fervent in spirit, and serving the Lord. The psalm was there, having the unceasing steadiness of the whole night, and always in the hands of the activity, and in the mouth of the divine psalm without diminution. The idler did not speak well there; The thought of gold and silver, or of any other thing, was not with them; the expense of the whole year, or the measure, or the meditations of a temporal life, appropriate to the pains, and the name was not known among them; but there was only one thing, first, which was hastened by all; so that everyone had died in the body, as once in the world, and had been put to death by those things which are in the world, and no longer living. But they had insufficient food, the words of the divinity; but they nourished the body with bread and water, so that they appeared much more effective in the presence of divine clemency.

CHAPTER 5.--This Zosimas, as he said, having insight, was greatly edified, aspiring to perfection, and making his own course of growth, finding his peers, and moving towards the divine paradise. After several days had passed, the time drew near, when it was customary for Christians to celebrate a sacred fast, and to purify themselves in order to greet the day of the divine passion and resurrection. But the royal monastery was never opened, but was always closed, and without any disturbance the monks completed their course; for it was not lawful to open it at any time, unless perhaps a monk came for some necessary work. For that place was lonely, and not only unusual, but also unknown to most of the neighbors. And such a canon was observed from ancient times: for which reason, as I consider, God led Zosimas into the same monastery.

CHAPTER 6.--After that I will relate how the tradition of the monastery itself was kept. On Sunday, which should be called the first week of fasting, the divine sacraments were performed as usual, and everyone became a partaker of the life-giving and undefiled body and blood of our Lord Jesus Christ. And having taken a little food as usual, they all assembled in the oratory, and with bowed knees, and made a supplicating prayer, they greeted each other as monks, and each kneeling publicly embraced the abbot, asking for prayer, that they might have him as a co-operator and companion in the struggle that had begun. With this behavior, the doors of the monastery were thrown open, and they chanted in unison: The Lord is my illumination and my salvation, whom shall I fear? Lord, defender of my life, from whom shall I be afraid? etc. (Ps. 26), they went out, often leaving one or two guardians of the monastery, not to guard what was stored inside (for there was nothing suitable for thieves among them), but not to leave the oratory without divine solemnities. But each one sold himself, according as he was able or wanted. For one was carrying a measure sufficient for the body, another acorns, another the fruit of palm trees, another vegetable infused with water, another nothing but his own body and the clothes he wore. And they were nourished, when the necessity of nature demanded, on the herbs which grew in the wilderness. But the canon was every man to himself, and the law without transgression, so that no one might know his partner, how he abstained, or how he acted. For as soon as they had crossed the Jordan, they sequestered themselves far from each other, and no one joined himself as a partner, valuing the city as solitude. But even if one of them saw someone coming towards him from a distance, he immediately turned back from his journey and went in another direction. And he lived for himself and for God, singing frequently and eating food at appointed times. Having thus celebrated all the fasts, they returned to the monastery before the life-giving day of the resurrection of our Lord and Savior Jesus Christ, which holy Sunday the holy Church accepted to celebrate with palm branches. And they returned, each one having his own consciousness as a witness of his own labor, knowing how he had worked, and what seeds of labor he had sown. And no one asked another in any way how or in what manner he had finished the struggle of labor.

CHAPTER 7.--This is therefore the canon of this monastery, and thus it was kept perfectly and very well. For each one, as has been said, was joined to God through solitude, and contended within himself, not to please men, but to God alone. For those things which are done for the sake of men, and which are done in order to please men, not only do not profit those who do them, but are also caused by many losses to those who do them. Then Zosimas therefore crossed the Jordan according to the usual law of the monastery, carrying with him a little something suitable for the needs of his body, and the clothes he used; and indeed he celebrated the canon, passing through the desert, and at the time of food, he met nature's need. And he sat at night on the ground, resting a little, and enjoying a little sleep, wherever the evening time found him. But he began to hasten early, always having the same unceasing purpose, having a desire, as he said, to enter into the desert, hoping to find some father living there, who could build him something, as he longed for, and he traveled without ceasing, as if he were with someone manifest hurrying A journey requiring twenty days, when the time of the sixth hour had arrived, he stopped a little way from the journey: and turning towards the East, he said his usual prayer. For he was accustomed to fix the course of his journey at an appointed time of day, and to stand and chant, and kneel down to pray. But while he was singing, and gazing intently into heaven, he saw on the right side, where he was praying, the shadow of a human body appearing; and at first he was troubled, and trembled, thinking that he had seen the imagination of some spirit; but, bracing himself with the sign of the cross, and throwing away fear from himself (for the end of his prayer was now pressing), turning his eyes, he saw someone in truth hastening to the part of the West. And there was a woman, it seemed, with a very black body, blackened by the heat of the sun, and having hair on her head as white as wool, small and straight, no more than descending to the nape of her neck.

CHAPTER 8.--So Zosimas seeing this, and being delighted with the desired sweetness, began to run hastily in that direction, where something else that appeared was hastening. For he rejoiced with great joy. For in the space of those days he had not seen the form of man, or of animals, or of birds or beasts. For he longed to know what or what kind of beast it was that was seen, hoping that the march of some one of his elders would be accomplished. But when she saw Zosima coming on the opposite side, she began to run away in the lower wilderness. But Zosimas, forgetting his old age, and not considering the labor of the journey, ran on at a very rapid pace, longing to behold the fugitive. For here he was persecuted; but she was advancing. But Zosima's course was more rapid, and he was a little nearer. And when he approached, so that his voice could already be heard, he began, uttering these words, to cry to Zosimas with tears: Why do you flee from me, a degenerate and a sinner, servant of God? Truly support me through God, whoever you are, for whose name you inhabit this wilderness. Support me, weak and unworthy. Support me for the hope that you have for the reward of such a labor. Stand and give prayer and blessing to the old man through God, who has never rejected anyone. With tears in Zosima's request, they came running to a certain place, in which a torrent was designated as if dry, in which he considered that there had been a torrent; but that place is such that it has a resemblance to how it appeared in that land. When they arrived at the aforesaid place, that which was fleeing descended, and ascended again in another direction. But Zosimas, crying and unable to advance anywhere, stood on the other side of the torrent, which seemed to have the appearance of a torrent, and added tears to tears, and increased his sighs with sighs, so that he could hear much more from the nearby noise of mourning.

CHAPTER 9.--Then that body which was fleeing, uttered such a voice: Abba Zosimas, forgive me for God's sake, since I cannot reveal myself to you when I am converted. For I am a woman, and naked of all bodily covering, as you see, and having the indecency of the body covered. But if you really want to offer prayer to a sinful woman, throw me the garment with which you are surrounded, so that I can cover the woman's weakness by turning to you, and I will accept your prayers. Then Zosimas was seized with trembling and excessive fear and excess of mind. For that man was very energetic, and very prudent by the gift of divinity, and he knew that he would not have called him by name whom he had never seen, and of whom he had never heard, unless the grace of providence had been most clearly enlightened. But he did with haste as he was commanded, and taking off the cloak in which he was clothed, threw himself towards him behind. She took it, covering as much as she could the part of the body which should be more covered than the rest, girded herself, and turning to Zosima, said to him: What did you think, Abba, of seeing a sinful woman? What do you want to see or learn from me, because you have not been so slow to endure labor? And he, prostrating himself on the ground, asked to receive the blessing according to custom. But he prostrated himself and she, and both of them lay on the ground, one asking for a blessing from the other.

CHAPTER X.--After many hours the woman said to Zosima: "Abba Zosima, it is yours to bless and pray; for you are supported by the honor of the presbytery, and for many years you have attended the holy altar, and you have been privy to the secret gifts of Christ's divinity." These words put Zosima into great fear and struggle, and the trembling old man was dripping with sweat. And he said to her, tired of his strength, and as if he had already caught his breath: "You are indeed already manifest from the very vision, O spiritual mother, since you have gone to the Lord, and you have died in a stronger part. But the most obvious tribute of all is your grace, that you should call me by a name which you have never seen. But since grace is not recognized by dignity, but is usually signified by the actions of souls, bless for God's sake, and give prayer for the fulfillment of your indulgence." And with the stability of the old saint, he said: "Blessed is the Lord, who secures the salvation of souls;" and Zosima answered "Amen," and both of them arose from the ground. And the old woman said: Man, why have you come to me, a sinner? However, since the grace of the Holy Spirit has indeed directed you to render some service suitable to the body of my smallness, tell me, how are the most Christian tribes governed today, how are the emperors, how is the flock of the holy Church fed? And Zosimas answered with this word: Mother, by your holy prayers God has granted a stable peace; but accept the consolation of the unworthy monk, and pray through the Lord for the whole world, and for me, a sinner, that the labor of this course and journey may not become for me a path of so much solitude without fruit. And she answered him: It is indeed for you, Abba Zosimas, as I have said, having the honor of the priesthood, to pray for all and for me, for to this you were also called; but since we have the commandment of obedience, which was commanded me by you, I will do good with my will. And having said these things, turning towards the East, and lifting up his eyes on high, and extending his hands, he began to pray with only the movement of his lips in silence, and his voice was not heard at all so that it could be understood. Wherefore even Zosimas could not recognize any words from the speech itself. And he stood, as he said, trembling, gazing at the ground, and speaking nothing at all. And he swore, offering God as witness of the word, because as he saw her persevering in the constancy of prayer, with her eyes raised a little from the sight of the earth, he saw her raised as if one cubit from the earth, and suspended in the air praying. And when he saw this, he was seized with great terror, prostrated himself on the ground, profuse with perspiration, and greatly frightened, and did not presume to say anything, but said to himself: Lord, have mercy on me.

CHAPTER 10.--After many hours the woman said to Zosima: Abba Zosima, it is yours to bless and pray; for you are supported by the honor of the presbytery, and for many years you have attended the holy altar, and you have been privy to the secret gifts of Christ's divinity. These words put Zosima into great fear and struggle, and the trembling old man was dripping with sweat. And he said to her, tired of his strength, and as if he had already caught his breath: You are indeed already manifest from the very vision, O spiritual mother, since you have gone to the Lord, and you have died in a stronger part. But the most obvious tribute of all is your grace, that you should call me by a name which you have never seen. But since grace is not recognized by dignity, but is usually signified by the actions of souls, bless for God's sake, and give prayer for the fulfillment of your indulgence. And with the stability of the old saint, he said: Blessed is the Lord, who secures the salvation of souls; and Zosima answering Amen, both of them arose from the ground. And the old woman said: Man, why have you come to me, a sinner? However, since the grace of the Holy Spirit has indeed directed you to render some service suitable to the body of my smallness, tell me, how are the most Christian tribes governed today, how are the emperors, how is the flock of the holy Church fed? And Zosimas answered with this word: Mother, by your holy prayers God has granted a stable peace; but accept the consolation of the unworthy monk, and pray through the Lord for the whole world, and for me, a sinner, that the labor of this course and journey may not become for me a path of so much solitude without fruit. And she answered him: It is indeed for you, Abba Zosimas, as I have said, having the honor of the priesthood, to pray for all and for me, for to this you were also called; but since we have the commandment of obedience, which was commanded me by you, I will do good with my will. And having said these things, turning towards the East, and lifting up his eyes on high, and extending his hands, he began to pray with only the movement of his lips in silence, and his voice was not heard at all so that it could be understood. Wherefore even Zosimas could not recognize any words from the speech itself. And he stood, as he said, trembling, gazing at the ground, and speaking nothing at all. And he swore, offering God as witness of the word, because as he saw her persevering in the constancy of prayer, with her eyes raised a little from the sight of the earth, he saw her raised as if one cubit from the earth, and suspended in the air praying. And when he saw this, he was seized with great terror, prostrated himself on the ground, profuse with perspiration, and greatly frightened, and did not presume to say anything, but said to himself: Lord, have mercy on me.

CHAPTER 12.--Having said this, but also many other things, the woman lifting him up, said: I am truly ashamed, forgive me, my abbot, to tell you the shame of my actions; yet since thou hast seen my naked body, I will lay bare to thee the works of my deeds, that thou mayest know how filthy lust and shame my soul is filled with confusion. For it is not, as you yourself have considered, for the sake of any glory that is around me, that I want to tell. For what shall I be able to boast, that I was made a vessel of the devil's choice? But I know that if I begin to tell the things that are about me, you will flee from me, as one flees from the face of a serpent, not being able to hear with his ears, because of the inexhaustible things I have done. But I will say, denying nothing, but I will report more truly, beseeching you first not to fail to pray for me, that I may merit mercy and find it on the day of judgment. And the old man, overflowing with tears, wept. Then the woman began to tell the things about herself, saying thus:

CHAPTER 13.--I, Father, indeed had a country in Egypt: but while my parents were living, in the twelfth year of my age, I came to Alexandria, spurning their affection, and how indeed I had first violated my virginity, and how incessantly and insatiably I had fallen subdued by the vice of lust, I am ashamed to consider For this is not a short thing to say: but I will say it sooner, that you may know the insatiable ardor of my vice, which I had for the love of rapine. I spent seventeen and more years lying publicly in the flames of luxury. I did not lose my virginity because of anyone's gift; for I did not receive anything from some who were willing to give; for I considered this, inflamed with the fury of lust, to make him run further towards me, gratuitously fulfilling my desire for rapine and crime. Nor indeed should you consider that I did not accept anything for riches; for I lived by begging, or often by spinning tow. For, as I said, I had an insatiable desire, so that I wallowed endlessly in the dunghill of luxury. And this was appeasing to me, and I considered this my life, if I had perpetrated an incessant injury to nature. As I was leading my life in this way, I saw, in a season of high tide, a multitude of Libyans and Egyptians, as it were, flocking to the sea. So I found someone and asked: Where are these men hurrying who are running? And he said to me: Everyone is going up to Jerusalem because of the exaltation of the holy cross, which is celebrated after a few days as usual. And I said to him: Do you think they will accept me if I choose to go with them? And he said: If you have a boat, no one will stop you. I said to him: Truly, brother, I have neither fare nor expense. But I will go and get into one of the ships which they have hired. And though they refuse, I will deliver myself; for having my body in their power, they will receive it for hire. And therefore I desired to walk with them (my Abba, forgive me) so that I might have many co-workers in the passion of my lust.

CHAPTER 14.--I said to you, my old lord, forgive me, and do not compel me to say my confusion. For I tremble, the Lord knows, for these words of mine stain even the very air. And Zosimas, pouring the earth with tears, answered her: Say for God's sake, O my mother, say, and do not pass over the following of so salutary a narrative. And she, adding to the former narration, added these things: And that young man, hearing the obscurity of my words, went away laughing. And I, throwing down the spindle, which I held in my hand (for after a time it became necessary for me to hold it), ran to the sea, where I saw them running, and I saw some young men standing on the shore, about ten in number, short of body and of very active countenance, and for that which I it was pleasant, the best. There were also others who had already boarded the ships. But impudently, as was my custom, I threw myself into their midst, saying: Take me also with you wherever you go, for I will not be implacable to you. But by uttering more dirty words to others, I moved them all to laughter. But they, seeing my blushing motion, took me and carried me into the boat. From there we began our voyage. But what happened after this, how can I tell you, O man of God? What language can speak, or what ear is able to hear what was done in the boat or on the journey? how to sin and willing I forced the wretched unwilling. It is not a story to be told, but an indescribable, most wicked species, of which I was then the unfortunate mistress of the crimes produced. Therefore now be satisfied, for I am amazed how that sea of mine endured the luxuries of iniquity, how the earth did not open its mouth and sink me alive into hell, which led so many souls into the snare of death. But, as I think, my God, who wants no one to perish, but that all be saved (1 Tim. 2), required repentance. For he does not want the death of the sinner, but waits patiently, enduring conversion (Ezek. 18). And so we went up to Jerusalem with great haste; and indeed how many days before the festival I spent in the city, I occupied myself in the most wicked works, and worse. For I was not sufficient to the young men who were luxuriating with me in the sea and on the journey, but also by gathering together many other strangers and citizens in my criminal act, I defiled by seducing them.

CHAPTER 15.--But when the festival of the holy exaltation of the precious cross came, I indeed, as before, was present, leading the youth and capturing souls. But at the first hour of the morning I saw all flocking to the church with one accord. I also went, running with the runners, and came with them into the court of the temple; and when the hour of the exaltation of the divine cross came, I thrust and thrust, and repulsed in a certain way, hastening to enter with the people, I pressed up to the door of the temple with those who were entering, approaching with great labor and tribulation and I was unhappy: but when I wanted to enter, they all entered without hindrance , but some divine power prevented me, not allowing me to enter. I was soon repulsed, therefore, and cast out; and being thrown out, I found myself standing alone in the court. But considering that this should happen to me through the infirmity of a woman, and mixing myself again with others, I somehow exerted myself to enter, but in fact I labored in vain.

CHAPTER 16.--For when I reached the threshold of the track, everyone was received inside, having no obstacle, but he did not receive me alone; but as if a military crowd had been levied to shut off my access to the ingredients, so some sudden force prevented me, and I found myself again in the court. Having suffered this three or four times and trying to do it, and achieving nothing, despairing of the rest, and unable to advance any further (for my body had become very broken by the force of the compression), I withdrew and stood in a certain corner of the temple court; and scarcely ever, for what reason I forbade myself to see the tree of life, I returned to my thoughts. For he touched my mind and the eyes of my heart with the understanding of salvation, reflecting that the wickedness of my actions blocked the way for me to enter. And so I began to weep exceedingly, and to heave my breast, and uttering sighs from the depths of my heart, and weeping and wailing, I looked up at the place where I stood, the image of the holy Mother of God standing above, and I said, gazing at her and paying unswerving attention; Lady virgin, who gave birth to God according to the flesh, I know that it is neither fitting nor appropriate for me to worship your image so hideous or to contemplate with eyes polluted by so much dirt, which you acknowledge to be a virgin and chaste, who has an immaculate body and soul: it is just that I am lustful from your most pure the purity of chastity is to be abhorred and thrown away. However, since, as I have heard, it is for this effect that God is a man, whom you have begotten worthy of, to call sinners to repentance, help me, who is alone and having no helper, understand my confession, and grant me permission to enter the church's open entrance, and I will not be made a stranger to by the vision of the most precious tree, in which the man God was affixed, whom thou didst conceive by a virgin, and gave his own blood for my deliverance. Command, O Lady, that the door be opened to me unworthy of the salutation of the divine cross, and I give you a pledge worthy of the Christ born of you, because I will never further defile my flesh by the horrible games of immiseration; but soon as your children, holy Virgin, I will see the tree, the world and its acts, and I will renounce all that is in it, and I will immediately go out wherever you lead me as a surety.

CHAPTER 17.--Having said this, and as if receiving some satisfaction, inflamed with the heat of faith, and presuming on the bowels of God's maternal piety, I moved from the same place where I stood and made my prayer; and coming, I mingled with those entering again, and there was no longer anyone to repel me, nor anyone to prevent me from approaching the doors by which they entered the temple. I was then seized with a strong tremor and ecstasy, and I was completely disturbed by the trembling of everything. And so, conjoining myself to the door, the access to which was at first barred to me (as if all the power which at first prevented me from entering, but afterwards prepared the way for me to enter), thus I entered without hindrance, and thus found myself within the holy of holies, and adored the mystery of the precious and life-giving wood of the cross I was considered worthy: and then I saw the sacraments of God, and how he is prepared to receive penitents. Then, throwing myself face down on the ground, and kissing that holy floor, I went out. But running to her who had trusted me, I came and stayed. I then joined myself in that place where the signature of trust was written, and bending the knee before the face of the holy Virgin Mother of God, I cursed myself with these words: Indeed, you always, O most kind Lady, showed your mercy of piety: you did not reject unworthy supplication; I saw the glory which we sinners do not see, the glory of Almighty God who through you accepts the penance of sins. What more sinful and wretched can I remember or tell? Now is the time to fulfill what I promised, by the faith of your love. Now send me where it pleases you. Be thou to me a guide of salvation, and a teacher of truth, going before me on the way which leads to repentance. And when he said these things, I heard the voice of someone crying from afar: If you cross the Jordan, you will find a good rest. But I, hearing this voice, and believing that it was done for me, cried out with tears, and looking forward to the image of the Mother of God I cried out: Lady, Lady, Queen of the whole world, through whom salvation has come to the human race, do not forsake me. And having said these things, I went out of the court of the temple, and walked hastily. And as I was going out, someone saw me and gave me three coins, saying: Take these, grandmother. I asked him who was selling bread: Where and what kind of road is known, man, which leads to the Jordan? And knowing the gate of the city which is on that side, I ran and wept.

CHAPTER 18.--And attaching question to question, I spent the rest of the day hastening on my way: but it was three o'clock in the morning, when I deserved to see the precious and holy cross. And when the sun was already setting, I beheld the church of the blessed John the Baptist, situated near the Jordan; And I communicated the living and undefiled sacraments of Christ the Lord, in the same holy church of the forerunner and John the Baptist, and then I ate half of one loaf and drank from the water of the Jordan, resting on the ground at night. At dawn on the morrow I passed into another direction, and again asked my guide to direct me where she pleased. And I came into this wilderness, and from that time until this day I have fled away, waiting for my God, who saves the small and the great who turn to him (Psal. 15). Zosimas said to her: How many years, O lady, since you have inhabited this desert? The woman answered: It is forty-seven years, as I consider, since I left the holy city. And Zosimas said: And what could you find to eat, O my, or you find, Lady. The woman answered: Indeed, I carried two loaves of bread across the Jordan; and those who, after a little withering, became as hard as stones, and I passed eating a little, until some years ago. And Zosimas said: And thus without pain have you passed such a length of time? Did you feel any sudden change and disturbance in the heat? She said: You are now asking me a matter, which I shudder to say, if I come to the remembrance of so many dangers which I have endured, and of the thoughts which unjustly troubled me: for I fear lest I should suffer some tribulation from them. Zosimas said: Leave nothing, O lady, that you do not mention. For once we have known you in this clear order, we must teach you all things in detail.

CHAPTER 19.--And she said to him: Believe me, abbot, for seventeen years I struggled with wild, untamed and irrational desires, while I initiated food, my desire was flesh; I coveted the fish that Egypt had; I longed also for wine that was pleasant to me; for I had great delight in wine, and I drank more abundantly to the point of drunkenness, and now I was very longing for the fact that I should use much while I was in the world. But here, having no water at all, I burned most violently, and endured the danger of necessity. I also had a great longing for luxurious songs, disturbing and bringing back to the memory of singing the songs of demons, which I had dedicated in the age. But presently, weeping, and beating my breast, I recalled to myself the fitting trust I had made in going out against this desert. Now I came by knowledge before the image of the holy Mother of God, who accepted me in her faith, and I wept before her, that the thoughts which afflicted my most miserable soul might flee from me. But when I was weeping excessively and painfully, and beating my breast manfully, then I saw a light shining all around me, and a kind of stable serenity soon became for me. But the thoughts which compelled me again to fornication, how can I tell you? Abba, forgive me. The fire inside my unhappy body was burning too much, and it was burning me all over, and it was dragging me to the desire of commotion. While such a thought occurred to me, I prostrated myself on the ground, and pouring tears into the earth, hoping that she would truly be the one who had trusted me, threatening to exaggerate me with an appeal, furious, as if transgressing, and threatening me with the punishments of transgression. For I had not before arisen from the earth, unless first that sweetest light had illuminated me as usual, and had driven away the thoughts which troubled me. Therefore I always raised the eyes of my heart to that my confidant without ceasing, imploring her to help me in this solitude and penance. I therefore had a helper and co-helper, the very one who gave birth to the author of chastity, and thus, during the course of seventeen years, with many dangers, as I have said, I have struggled to this day. From that time, therefore, my helper, the mother of God, stood by me, guiding me through everything in everything. And Zosimas said: Have you not had food or clothing? And she said: Indeed, as I have already said, I spent seventeen years on those breads, and then fed them with herbs that were found in the wilderness. But the garment which I had, having passed over the Jordan, was torn and worn out with great age. Therefore I endured much necessity with the icy cold and the heat of the heat, I was crushed by the scorching heat, and at the time of the great trinity I was frozen and shivering with frost, many times falling to the ground without breath I lay motionless, struggling with many and various needs and immense temptations, through everything until this day the power of God is many He saved my poor soul and my body in many ways. Remembering from what evils the Lord has delivered me, I feed on inexhaustible food, and I possess the food of satiety, the hope of my salvation. But I am nourished and covered by the shelter of the word of God, which contains all things (Deut. 8). For man does not live on bread alone (Matt. 3), and not having a covering of rock, those who have stripped themselves of their coat of sin are surrounded by a covering (Job 24, juxta 70).

CHAPTER 20.--Now Zosimas hearing that he was bringing forth the testimonies of the Scriptures, namely from the books of Moses and the blessed Job, or from the Psalms, said to her: Have you learned the Psalms, O mother, or have you read other books of the Holy Scriptures? And she, hearing this, smilingly said to him: Believe me, I have not seen a man from whence I crossed the Jordan, but you this day; But I never learned literature anywhere, but neither did I listen to anyone singing or reading. But the living and effective word of God teaches the inner understanding of man. (Heb. 4). This is the end of what is mine. And now, beseeching you, through the incarnation of the Word of God, to be a mouthful for me. And when he had said these things, the old man ran and bowed his knees to the ground, crying out and saying: Blessed be the Lord God, who alone does great wonders, glorious and exceedingly astonishing, of which there is no number (Job 9). Blessed art thou, Lord God, who hast shown me how great a gift thou givest to those who fear thee. For indeed Thou wilt not forsake those who seek Thee, O Lord (Psal. 9). But she, taking hold of the old man, did not allow him to fall completely prostrate on the ground, but said to him: These things you have heard, man, I warn you through the Lord our Savior Jesus Christ, you will not tell anyone until God releases me from the bond of the flesh. Having received all these in peace, and again at this same time in the coming year, I will appear to you, and you will see me, the grace of God guiding us. But do for the Lord's sake what I command you now, so that you do not cross the Jordan during the recurring sacred fasts of the year to come, as you have a custom in the monastery. But Zosimas was amazed, hearing that the canon of the monastery was ignorant, as if he knew what he was saying; and he cried out for nothing but the glory of God, who bestows upon the diligent more than is asked. And she said: Stay as I said, abbot, in the monastery; and even if you want to go out anywhere, you will not be able to. And in the evening of the most sacred supper of Sunday, bring a portion of the divine body and life-giving blood in a sacred vessel worthy of so great a mystery, and support me on the side of the Jordan which is joined to the world, and coming to life I may receive gifts. For from the time that I took part in the church of the most blessed Forerunner, before I crossed the Jordan, I have never taken part in it until now, I have never until now used a portion of this sanctification; and therefore, I beseech you, do not reject my request, but by all means revive and bring the divine mysteries at that hour when the Lord made the disciples partakers of the divine supper. And to John, the abbot of the monastery in which you live, say: Take care of yourself and your flock; for there are some things that stand in need of correction. But I do not want you to tell him these things now, but when God has commanded you. Saying these things, and demanding prayer from the old man, he hastened more quickly into the interior solitude.

CHAPTER 21.--And Zosimas prostrated himself, kissed the place of the earth on which his footprints stood, giving glory to God: and giving immense thanks, he returned, praising and blessing the Lord our God Jesus Christ. And retrieving again the same lonely road by which he had come, he joined in the monastery at the time which was customary for those who stayed in the same. And indeed he remained silent that whole year, not at all daring to say anything of what he had seen; but inwardly he implored God to show him again the desirable face. But he sighed, considering the slowness of the year's course. But when the sacred fasts, initiated on the first Sunday, arrived, immediately after the usual prayer others came out singing; but he himself, seized with a slight illness of fever, remained inside the monastery. But Zosimas remembered what that saint had said to him, that you will not be able to go out unwillingly. But after a few days had passed, he was relieved from his infirmity, and spent his time in a monastery. When the monks had returned in the evening of the consecrated supper, he did as he was commanded: and putting in a little chalice a portion of the undefiled body and precious blood of our Lord Jesus Christ, he put in a basket a few caricas and the fruits of palms, that is, dactyls, and a little lentils steeped in water; and he came slowly, and sat by the bank of the Jordan, longing for the coming of the holy one. And that most blessed woman of slowness, Zosimas did not slumber, but attentively attended to the solitude, enduring what he longed to see. And he said to himself: Did she come back when she did not find me? Saying these things, he wept; and lifting up his eyes to heaven, he implored God supplicatingly, saying: Let not strangers see me again, O Lord, as thou hast given me to see. I will not go empty-handed, bearing my sins in rebuke.

CHAPTER 22.--While he was praying with tears, another thought occurred to him. What then, if he comes, will he do? how will he cross the Jordan, since there is no boat? How shall the unworthy reach me? Alas, wretched me! Alas,

THE LIFE OF ST. MARY OF EGYPT

who has alienated me from such a fair appearance? While the old man was thinking this, behold, the holy woman came, and stood on the other side of the river from whence she had come. But Zosimas, seeing her, got up rejoicing, and exulting greatly glorified God. But the struggle of the struggle was fluctuating in his thought, because he cannot cross the flowing Jordan. And the old man looking up, saw her marking the waters of the Jordan with the banner of the cross. For at that time all the darkness of the night was illumined by the brightness of the moon, because it was the time of her return. And as soon as he had made the sign of the cross, he ascended upon the waters; and walking on a liquid wave of water, he came as if by a solid path. But Zosimas, astonished, and endeavoring to bend his knees, cried out from above, and stopped the waters, saying: What are you doing, abbot, since you are also a priest of God, and you carry the divine mysteries? He immediately obeyed what was said. And she, descending from the waters, said to the old man: Bless, Father, bless. But he answered with great haste (for astonishment had overtaken him too much at such a glorious miracle), and said: Truly God does not lie, who has promised that those who purify themselves will be like him. Glory to you, Christ our God, who showed me through this handmaid of yours, how far below my own consideration I am the measure of true perfection. Saying these things, the woman demanded that he say the holy Symbol, and thus begin the Sunday prayer. And when he had finished, our holy Father, as is the custom, offered the elder a kiss of peace; and thus revives the mysteries, receiving the gifts, stretching out his hands to heaven, groaning with tears, thus crying out: Now, O Lord, let your handmaid go in peace according to your word; because my eyes have seen your salutation (Luke 2). And he said to the old man: Forgive me, Abba, and fulfill another commandment of my request. Go now to the monastery, guided by the peace of God; but at the end of the coming year I came again in that torrent, in which I spoke with you before. Do not forsake me through all things, but I have come for God's sake: and you will see me again, as God wills. And he answered her: Would that it were possible now to follow your steps, and enjoy the sight of your most precious face! I pray, mother, that you will make one small petition for the old man, and that you will deign to accept a little food from what I have brought here. And saying these things, he showed him that he had brought the basket with him. She, with her last fingers, touched a lentil, and taking three grains, brought them to her own mouth, saying that the grace of the Spirit was sufficient to preserve the immaculate substance of the soul. Then he says to the old man: Pray for me for God's sake, and always be mindful of my unhappiness. He, touching her holy feet, begged her with tears to pray for the Church, and for the government, and for himself, and thus he sent her away weeping and wailing. For he did not dare to detain her much, which could not be detained even if he wished.

CHAPTER 23.--And that cross again signing the Jordan, he went up walking on the liquid element, and passed over as he had done before. But the old man returned filled with joy and trembling. And he reproached himself, repenting, because he did not inquire into the holy name in order to know it; he still hoped to achieve this in the coming year.

CHAPTER 24.--And when the course of the same year had passed, he came again into the vast wilderness of the desert, having finished all according to custom, he hastened to gaze upon that glorious vision. But wandering through the desert, and not finding any signs indicating the place he desired, he looked to the right and to the left, leading the sight of his eyes, and scanning everywhere like the swiftest hunter, wherever he seized the sweetest beast. But as he saw nothing moving in any way, he began to mourn himself and pour out tears. Then raising his eyes, he prayed, saying: I beseech you, Lord, show me in the body an angel, to whom the whole world is unworthy to be compared.

CHAPTER 25.--While he was praying, he arrived at the place which had been designated in the likeness of a torrent, and in the extreme upper part of it he saw the shining sun; and looking, he saw the body of the saint lying dead, and the hands, as it should be, thus joined, and the body lying looking towards the East. And running, he washed the feet of the most blessed with tears, for he dared not touch any other member of his body. After weeping for some time, and reciting psalms appropriate to the time and the matter, he made the funeral oration, and said to himself: Perhaps it will not please the holy to do these things. With this in mind, there was a designated writing on the ground, where it read: "Bury, Abba Zosimas, the little body of poor Mary." Give back to the earth what is its own, and add dust to dust. Pray only for me, for the Lord's sake, in the passing month of Parmoth, according to the Egyptians; which according to the Romans is on the ninth day of April, that is, the 5th day of April of the salutary passion, after the communion of the divine and sacred supper."

CHAPTER 26.--When the old man had read these letters, he thought first who it was who had written them: for she, as he had said, was ignorant of letters. In this, however, he rejoiced exceedingly, because he had learned his holy name. He thought, indeed, that as soon as he had partaken of the divine mysteries in the Jordan, at the same hour he came to that place, where he had just passed from this world, and the same journey which Zosimas had hardly completed by walking for twenty days, laboring, had been completed in the course of one hour by Mary, and immediately went to Master. And Zosimas glorifying the Lord, and pouring tears over his body: It is time, says he, poor Zosimas, to do what is yours. But what shall I do, the unhappy man, because I have no means of digging? There is no hoe, there is no rake, and I have nothing of all at hand. Saying these things to him in his heart, he saw a small piece of wood lying there; assuming that, he began to dig. But the earth was very hard, and very strong, and it was by no means worth digging, because both being exhausted by fasting and the fatigue of the long journey, the deficiency was too great. For he labored, and was pressed by excessive sighs, and wet with perspiration, he groaned heavily from the very depths of his heart. And looking back, he saw a lion of enormous form standing near the body of the saint, and licking its plants. And when they saw it, they trembled with terror at that great beast, especially because they had heard that holy woman say that she had never seen any beast. And with the sign of the cross he confirmed himself on every side, believing that the virtue of lying was able to keep him unharmed. But Leo began to beckon the old man, saluting him with flattering nods. And Zozimas said to the lion: Because you have been sent by God, most of the beasts, that the body of this handmaiden of God may be commended to the earth, fulfilling the work of duty, so that his little body may be buried. For I, being worn out in old age, am not able to dig, but neither have I anything suitable to perform this work; and again I am not able to hasten the length of the journey to bring it. You, by divine command, do this work with your hooves, so that we may commend this holy little body to the earth.

CHAPTER 27.--Continuing, next to the conversation of the old man, the lion himself made a pit with his arms, large enough to bury the body of the saint. But the old man, washing the feet of the saint with tears, and pouring out many prayers, exhorting her for all then and more for himself, covered the earth with her naked body, standing by the lion, as he had found her before, and having nothing else but the torn garment which he had already thrown to her before. Zosimas, from whom Mary covered certain parts of her body. Then they retired together; and indeed the lion went into the interior of solitude like a tame sheep; But Zosimas returned, blessing and praising God, and singing a hymn of praise to Christ our Lord. And when he came to the convent, he told them all from the beginning, and hid nothing of all that he saw and heard, so that all who heard the great things of God were astonished with great astonishment, and with fear and love celebrated with great faith the day of the most blessed holy passage. But John the abbot found some in need of correction, according to the words of that saint, and these, having mercy on the Lord God, he converted. And Zosimas, dwelling in the same monastery, completed a hundred years, and then departed to the Lord in peace, by the grace of our Lord Jesus Christ, to whom with the Father be glory and honor and dominion together with the holy life-giving and adoring Spirit, now and ever and unto ages of ages. Amen.

LATIN TEXT

THE LIFE OF ST. MARY OF EGYPT

PRAEFATIO INTERPRETIS.

Domino gloriosissimo ac praestantissimo regi Carolo.

Sciens gloriosissimam majestatem vestram tam divinis eloquiis, quam sanctorum praecedentium exemplis valde delectari, cum jamdudum libellum conversionis Mariae Aegyptiacae, cum tomulo de cujusdam vicedomini poenitentia, domino meo obtulerim, quia ille ipse casu quodam deperiit, nunc interim jussui vestro in eodem restaurando devotus obedivi. Obsequii quoque et devotionis meae fuit ut non simplicem tantum memoratae rei textum exhiberem, sed et alia quaesitu digna superadjicerem, de venerandis scilicet constitutis et gestis praesulum Romanae Ecclesiae: quorum sanctionibus quam reverenter Ecclesia utatur, majestas vestra optime novit. Hoc autem brevitatis compendium servus vester ideo sumpsit, ut serenitas vestra, quam Reipublicae fascibus valde oneratam attendo, cui sparsim diversa non vacat percurrere scriptorum volumina, quasdam consuetudines ecclesiasticas in brevi, quasi in quodam Enchiridio inclusas, tenere possit, et quia secundum regalem industriam studium domini mei in hoc fervere didici, ut facta dictave vestra juxta auctoritatem irrefragabilem dirigere, et quid erga cultum divinum tenendum, quidve rejiciendum sit, sollicite disquirere et perscrutari, elucubrationis sit assiduae, qualiter ejus divinitatis ope muniti, prosperis successibus ad omnia currere mereamini.

Prologus auctoris.

Secretum regis celare, bonum est; opera autem Dei revelare et confiteri, honorificum est (Tob. XII). Ita enim legitur, angelum dixisse Tobiae post oculorum amissionem, gloriosamque illuminationem, et post illa transacta pericula, e quibus liberatus, consecutus est Dei pietatem. Etenim regis secretum manifestare, nocivum et valde periculosum est; et Dei gloriosa silere opera, magnum est animae detrimentum. Propter quod ego divina tegere silentio dubitans, et pigri servi metuens condemnationis imminens judicium, qui a domino talentum accipiens, fodiens in terram abscondit, et datum ad operationem celavit extra negotiationem (Matth. XXV), sacram ad me prolatam narrationem nequaquam silebo. Sed nullus mihi sit incredulus scribenti de eis quae audivi, nec quisquam me mentiri aestimet, de rei magnitudine dubitans. Mihi enim absit sacris mentiri rebus, et adulterari verbum, ubi Deus memoratur. Ejus autem, qui minima intelligit, et indignius de Dei magnitudine, qui carnem assumpsit, et incredulus est ista dicenti, non mihi pertinebit periculum. Si qui autem illi sunt qui hujus scripturae legerint textum, gloriosamque rei admirationem sane credere renuerint, et illis Dominus misereatur, faciatque capaces sancti verbi, ne rei existant Dei miraculorum, quae plura in suis fieri praedestinavit electis: quoniam et ipsi humanae naturae infirma considerantes, impossibilia decernunt ea quae de hominibus sanctis gloriosa dicuntur. Assumam de caetero narrationem, ipsam rem referens, quae in hac nostra generatione facta dignoscitur, quam sacer vir, divina et agere et docere educatus, narravit. Sed ut supra dictum est, nullus haec ad incredulitatem trahat, considerans impossibile fieri in hac nostra generatione tam grande miraculum, quia gratia Dei per omnes generationes in sanctas pertransiens animas, amicos Dei facit et prophetas, quemadmodum Salomon secundum Deum edocuit (Sap. VII). Tempus namque est sacrae prodere narrationis initium, magnum virileque certamen venerabilis Mariae Aegyptiacae, videlicet qualiter expleverit tempora vitae suae.

VITA.

CAPUT PRIMUM.--In monasterio Palaestinorum fuit vir vitae moribus et verbo ornatus, qui ab ipsis cunabulis, monachicis est actibus diligenter instructus, et conversationibus veraciter educatus, nomine Zosimas. Et nullus nos aestimet dicere Zosimam illum in praedicationis erroneae dogmatibus accusatum sectae alterius; alius enim hic, et alius ille, et multa inter utrosque distantia, licet unum uterque sortiti sint vocabuli nomen. Hic itaque Zosimas ab initio in uno Palaestinorum conversatus est monasterio, et omnem pertransiens monachicam disciplinam, in abstinentiae opere omnium factus est probatissimus. Omne enim praeceptum sibi traditum canonis ab his qui ab infantia educati sunt, luctam perfectae disciplinae monachicae irreprehensibiliter conservabat. Multa etiam et ipse sibi adjiciens superaddidit, cupiens carnem spiritui subjugare. Nec enim in aliquo offendisse comprobatur. Ita enim fuit in cunctis perfectus monachicis actibus, ut multoties multi monachi de praedicti loci monasteriis et de longinquis partibus ad eum confluentes, ejus exemplis atque doctrinis se constringerent, et ad illius imitationem abstinentiae se multo magis subjugarent.

CAP. II.--Haec itaque omnia in se habens, a meditatione sacri eloquii nunquam discessit, sed in stratu suo quiescens, sive surgens, aut operam tenens manibus, vel cibum, si conveniebat ut sumeret, bonum, quo ille uti consueverat, spiritualiter utebatur, unum opus habebat intacitum et nunquam deficiens, psallere frequenter et meditationem facere sacri eloquii. Multoties enim asserunt quia et divinae illustrationis dignus effectus, a Deo sibi visiones ostensae sunt, et mirum non est nec incredibile. Si enim, ut ait Dominus, beati mundo corde, quoniam ipsi Deum videbunt (Matth. V); quanto magis qui suam purificaverint carnem, sobrii semper, animorumque pervigiles, oculos divinae prospiciunt illustrationis, visionis indicium hinc praeparatae futurae bonitatis accipientes? Dicebat autem ipse Zosimas, ab ipsis, ut ita dicam, maternis ulnis in hoc se esse monasterio traditum, et usque ad quinquagesimum tertium annum in eo cursum monachicum peregisse. Post haec autem pulsatus est a quibusdam cogitationibus, quasi jam in omnibus esset perfectus, alterius non indigens in ullo doctrina. Haec autem, ut dicebat, in se cogitabat: Nunquid est in terris monachus, qui novum aliquid possit tradere mihi, juvare me valens in aliquo quod ignorem, aut quod ego in monachico non expleverim opere? Nunquid invenitur eorum qui solitudinem duxerunt vir qui prior me in actibus sit? Haec et his similia eo cogitante, astitit quidam et dixit ei: O Zosima, bene quidem, et sicut possibile fuit homini, decretasti, bene cursum monachicum consummasti. Tamen nullus est in hominibus qui se perfectum esse demonstret. Major enim lucta praesens quam illa quae praeteriit, licet tu nescias. Ut autem cognoscas quantae sint et aliae viae salutis, egredere de terra et de cognatione tua, et de domo patris tui, ut Abraham ille patriarcharum eximius (Gen. XII), et veni ad monasterium quod juxta Jordanem adjacet flumen.

CAP. III.--Mox igitur secutus dicentem, egressus de monasterio, in quo ab infantia conversatus est, et perveniens ad Jordanem, fluvium omnium sanctiorem, dirigitur ab eo qui vocavit eum in monasterium in quod illum Deus venire praecepit. Pulsans igitur monasterii januam, loquitur prius monacho qui januam observabat, et ille nuntiavit eum abbati. Qui suscipiens eum, habituque et specie religiosum conspiciens, postquam flexit genu, ut mos est monachis, accepta oratione, hoc eum interrogavit: Unde frater, advenisti? et quam ob rem apud humiles te conjunxisti monachos? Zosimas autem respondit: Unde quidem veni, non puto necessarium dicere; aedificationis autem gratia, Pater, adveni. Audivi de vobis magnalia et laude digna, et posse Deo animam sociare. Dixit autem ei abbas: Deus, frater, qui solus sanat animae infirmitatem, ipse te et nos doceat divina mandata, et dirigat omnes ad ea facienda quae opportuna sunt. Homo enim hominem aedificare non valet, nisi unusquisque attendat semetipsum frequenter, et sobrio intellectu quod expedibile est operetur, Deum habens cooperatorem. Tamen quoniam, ut dixisti, charitas Christi te videre nos humiles monachos perduxit, mane nobiscum, si ob hoc venisti, ut omnes nos nutriet pastor bonus sancti Spiritus sui gratia, qui animam suam dedit liberationem pro nobis, et proprias oves vocat ex nomine (Matth. XX; Joan. X). Haec dicente abbate, flectens iterum Zosimas genua, accepta oratione, respondit Amen, et mansit in eodem monasterio.

CAP. IV.--Vidit autem ibi seniores actibus et visione splendentes, spiritu ferventes, et Domino servientes. Psallentia ibi erat, incessabiles totius noctis habens stabilitates, et in manibus semper operatio, et in ore psalmi divini absque diminutione. Sermo ibi otiosus non proficiebat; cogitatio auri argentique, aut rei alicujus apud illos non erat; expensa anni totius, aut mensura, vel temporalis vitae meditationes, doloribus congruae, nec nomen apud illos cognoscebatur; sed unum erat primum solummodo, quod festinabatur ab omnibus; ut unusquisque mortuus esset corpore, sicut semel saeculo, et eis quae in saeculo sunt mortificatus, et jam non vivens. Cibum autem habebant indeficientem, divinitatis eloquia; nutriebant vero corpus pane et aqua, ut multo magis apud divinam clementiam apparerent efficaces.

CAP. V.--Haec Zosimas, ut dicebat, perspiciens, aedificabatur valde, praetendens se ad perfectionem, et crescere faciens proprium cursum, cooperatores inveniens, optime divinum innovantes paradisum. Transactis autem aliquot diebus, appropinquavit tempus, quando sacra jejunia Christianis traditum est celebrare, et purificare seipsos ob divinae passionis diem resurrectionisque salutationem. Regia autem monasterii nunquam aperiebatur, sed semper erat clausa, et absque ulla perturbatione monachi cursum suum explebant; nec enim erat licitum aperire aliquando, nisi fortassis monachus propter aliquod opus necessarium adveniebat. Solitarius enim erat locus ille, et plurimis vicinorum non solum inusitatus, sed et incognitus. Canon autem talis a priscis servabatur temporibus: propter quod, ut considero, Deus Zosimam perduxit in idem monasterium.

CAP. VI.--Dehinc ergo referam qualiter ipsius monasterii servabatur traditio. Dominica quam primam jejuniorum hebdomadam nominari mos est, agebantur divina sacramenta consuete, et unusquisque particeps efficiebatur vivifici ac intemerati corporis et sanguinis Domini nostri Jesu Christi. Et solito modicum cibum sumentes, congregabantur omnes in oratorium, et curvatis genibus, factaque suppliciter oratione, salutabant se invicem monachi, et unusquisque genuflexo publice amplectebatur abbatem, postulantes orationem, ut haberent ad inchoatum certamen eum cooperatorem et comitatorem. His ita se habentibus, fores monasterii patefiebant, et psallentes consona voce: Dominus illuminatio mea et salus mea, quem timebo? Dominus defensor vitae meae, a quo trepidabo? etc. (Psal. XXVI), exibant, unum multoties aut duos monasterii custodes relinquentes, non ut custodirent ea quae intus erant reposita (non enim erant apud illos aliqua furibus congrua), sed ne oratorium absque divinis relinquerent solemniis. Unusquisque autem se annonabat, prout poterat aut volebat. Nam unus portabat corpori ad mensuram sufficiens, alius carycas, alius palmarum fructus dactylos, alius vero legumina aquis infusa, alius nihil praeter corpus proprium et vestimentum quo utebatur. Nutriebantur autem, quando necessitas exigebat naturae, herbis quae nascebantur per solitudinem. Canon autem erat unusquisque sibi ipsi et lex absque praevaricatione, ut non cognosceret aliquis consocium, qualiter abstinebat, aut quomodo agebat. Jordanem enim mox transmeantes, longe ab invicem se sequestrabant, et nullus se jungebat ad socium, civitatem aestimantes solitudinem. Sed et si unus ex ipsis a longe venientem ad se aliquem videbat, mox declinabat de itinere, et ad aliam partem pergebat. Vivebat autem sibi et Deo, psallens frequenter et constituto gustans tempore cibum. Ita omnia jejunia celebrantes, revertebantur ad monasterium ante vivificum diem resurrectionis Domini et Salvatoris nostri Jesu Christi, quam festam Dominicam cum ramis palmarum celebrare sancta accepit Ecclesia. Revertebantur autem, unusquisque habens proprii laboris testem propriam conscientiam, cognoscentem qualiter operatus est, et qualia laborum semina seminavit. Et nullus ullo modo interrogabat alium, quomodo aut qualiter laboris certamina consummasset.

CAP. VII.--Hic est itaque hujus monasterii canon, et ita perfecte et optime custodiebatur. Unusquisque enim, ut dictum est, per solitudinem Deo jungebatur, et in semetipso decertabat, ne hominibus placeret, sed soli Deo. Illa enim quae propter homines fiunt, et quae ut hominibus placeant aguntur, non solum non proderunt facientibus, sed et per multa damna efficiuntur agentibus obnoxia. Tunc itaque Zosimas consueta monasterii lege transmeavit Jordanem, modicum quid pro corporis necessitate deportans congrua, et vestem qua utebatur; et canonem quidem celebrabat, solitudinem pertransiens, et tempore escae necessitatem faciebat naturae. Sedebat autem nocte in terra, modicum quiescens, et somnum ad modicum gustans, quocunque eum vespertinum reperiebat tempus. Diluculo autem properare incipiebat, semper incessabile idem habens propositum, in desiderium habens, ut dicebat, introire in solitudinem, sperans invenire aliquem patrem in ea habitantem, qui eum posset aliquid aedificare, sicut desiderabat, et sine cessatione iter agebat, ac si apud aliquem manifestum festinans. Viginti autem dierum exigens iter, cum sextae horae tempus advenisset, stetit modicum ab itinere: et conversus ad Orientem, agebat solitam orationem. Consueverat enim constituto diei tempore figere itineris cursum, et stans psallere, et genuflexo orare. Dum autem psalleret, et in coelum inspiceret intentis obtutibus, vidit a parte dextra, ubi orabat, umbram quasi humani corporis apparentem; et primo quidem conturbatus est, ac contremuit, phantasiam alicujus spiritus existimans se vidisse, signo autem crucis se muniens, et a se timorem projiciens (jam enim et orationis ejus finis instabat), convertens oculos, vidit aliquem in veritate properantem ad partem Occidentis. Mulier autem erat, quod videbatur, corpore nigerrimo, prae solis ardore denigrata, et capillos capitis habens ut lana albos, modicos et ipsos, non amplius quam usque ad cervicem descendentes.

CAP. VIII.--Hoc itaque Zosimas videns, et desideratae dulcedinis gavisus effectus, coepit festinanter currere in eam partem, ubi et aliud quod apparuit festinabat. Gaudebat enim gaudio magno. Non enim viderat in spatio dierum illorum speciem hominis, aut animalium, vel volucrum, bestiarumque formam. Desiderabat enim cognoscere quae vel qualis bestia esset quae videbatur, sperans quoniam majorum alicujus efficeretur profectus. Illa autem ut vidit econtra Zosimam venientem, coepit fugiens currere apud inferiorem solitudinem. Zosimas autem aetatis senectam obliviscens, et laborem non reputans itineris, tetendit rapidissimo cursu, desiderans conspicere fugientem. Hic enim persequebatur; illa autem progrediebatur. Erat autem cursus Zosimae velocior, et paulo efficiebatur propinquior. Ubi autem appropiavit, ut jam etiam posset vox audiri, coepit, has voces emittens, clamare Zosimas cum lacrymis: Cur me fugis decrepitum ac peccatorem, serve Dei? Vere sustine me per Deum, quicunque es, pro cujus nomine hanc inhabitas solitudinem. Sustine me infirmum et indignum. Sustine me pro spe, quam habes pro tanti laboris remuneratione. Sta, et tribue orationem et benedictionem seni per Deum, qui neminem aliquando projecit. Haec cum lacrymis Zosima postulante, venerunt currentes in quemdam locum, in quo quasi aridus torrens designabatur, in quo fuisse torrentem consideravit; sed locus ille talem convenit, ut haberet similitudinem, quomodo in terra illa apparebat. Ut venerunt itaque in praedictum locum, illud quod fugiebat descendit, et iterum ascendit in partem aliam. Zosimas autem clamans et nusquam progredi valens, stetit in aliam partem torrentis, qui speciem videbatur habere torrentis, et addidit lacrymas lacrymis, et suspiria suspiriis ampliavit, ut multo magis ex propinquo stridore luctus audiret.

CAP. IX.--Tunc illud corpus quod fugiebat, vocem talem emisit: Abba Zosima, ignosce mihi propter Deum, quoniam manifestare me tibi conversa non possum. Mulier enim sum, et omni corporeo tegmine nuda, ut ipse vides, et corporis turpitudinem habens intectam. Sed si vis peccatrici mulieri orationem vere tribuere, projice mihi indumentum quo circumdatus es, ut possim muliebrem infirmitatem operire ad te convertens, et tuas accipiam orationes. Tunc tremor nimiusque metus et mentis excessus accepit Zosimam. Strenuus enim erat vir ille valde, et divinitatis dono prudentissimus, et cognovit quia ex nomine non vocasset eum quem nunquam viderat, de quo nec unquam audierat, nisi manifestissime providentiae gratia fuisset illustrata. Fecit autem cum festinatione quod jussum est, et exuens se pallio quo erat indutus, terga versus projecit ei. Illa accipiens, in quantum potuit tegens partem corporis, quam oportet plus tegi caeteris, praecinxit se, et conversa ad Zosimam, ait ei: Quid tibi visum est, abba, peccatricem videre mulierem? Quid quaeris a me videre aut discere, quia tantum non pigritasti tolerare laborem? Ille autem in terra prostratus, poscebat benedictionem secundum morem accipere. Prostravit autem se et ipsa, et utrique jacebant in terra, unus ex alio benedictionem poscens.

CAP. X.--Post multarum autem horarum spatia dixit mulier ad Zosimam: Abba Zosima, tibi competit benedicere et orare; tu enim presbyterii honore fultus es, et plurimis jam annis sancto assistis altari, et donis divinitatis Christi secreta rimaris. Haec verba Zosimam in magnum timorem et certamen magis inducebant, et tremens senex sudoris guttis infundebatur. Dicit autem ei defessus viribus et quasi halitu jam conclusus: Manifesta jam quidem es ex ipsa visione, o spiritualis mater, quoniam tu ad Dominum profecta es, et fortiori parte mortua es. Manifesta autem plus omnium tributa est tibi gratia, ut me vocares ex nomine, quem nunquam vidisti. Sed quia gratia non ex dignitate cognoscitur, sed ex animarum actibus significari consueta est, benedic propter Deum, et orationem tribue indulgentiae tuae perfectionis. Stabilitati autem senis sancti compassa, dixit: Benedictus Dominus, qui salutem procurat animarum; et Zosima respondente Amen, surrexerunt utrique de terra. Et ait mulier seni: Homo, quam ob rem ad me peccatricem venisti? Tamen quoniam quidem te gratia Spiritus sancti direxit, ut aliquod ministerium exhibeas meae exiguitatis corpori congruum, dic mihi, quomodo hodie Christianissima regitur tribus, quomodo imperatores, quomodo sanctae Ecclesiae pascitur grex? Zosimas autem respondit hoc verbum: Mater, tuis orationibus sanctis pacem stabilem Deus largitus est; sed suscipe indigni monachi consolationem, et per Dominum ora pro omni mundo, et pro me peccatore, ut non hujus cursus et itineris labor sine fructu mihi efficiatur tantae solitudinis via. Et illa respondit ad eum: Te quidem oportet, abba Zosima, sacerdotii, ut dixi, habentem honorem, pro omnibus et pro me orare, in hoc enim et vocatus es; sed quia obedientiae praeceptum habemus, quod mihi a te jussum est, bona faciam voluntate. Et haec dicens, ad Orientem conversa, et elevatis in excelsum oculis, manibusque extensis, coepit orare motu tantum labiorum in silentio, voxque penitus non audiebatur ut posset intelligi. Unde et Zosimas nulla potuit verba ex ipsa oratione agnoscere. Stabat autem, ut dicebat tremens, terram conspiciens, et nihil ullo modo loquens. Jurabat autem, Deum testem verbi proponens, quoniam ut vidit eam perseverantem in orationis constantia, paululum elevatis ab aspectu terrae oculis, vidit eam elevatam quasi cubitum unum a terra, et in aere pendentem orare. Hoc autem ut vidit, nimio pavore correptus, prostravit se in terram, sudore suffusus, et nimium perterritus, nihil dicere praesumebat, in seipso autem dicebat: Domine, miserere mei.

CAP. XI.--In terra autem prostratus jacens, scandalizabatur in mente, putans ne spiritus esset qui se fingeret orare. Conversa autem mulier, erexit monachum dicens: Quid te, abba, cogitationes tuae perturbant scandalizari in me, quia spiritus sum, et fictam orationem facio? Satisfactus esto, homo, peccatricem me esse mulierculam, tamen sacro sum circumdata baptismate; et non sum spiritus, sed favilla et cinis et totum caro, et nihil spiritualis phantasiae aliquando vel ad mentem reducens. Haec dicens, signo crucis signat frontem suam, oculosque et labia; simulque et pectori vexillum crucis infigens, ita dixit: Deus, abba Zozima, de adversario et immissionibus ejus liberet nos, quoniam multa super nos est invidia ejus. Haec audiens senex, prosternit se, et apprehendit pedes ejus, dicens cum lacrymis: Obsecro te per Dominum Jesum Christum, verum Dominum nostrum, qui de virgine nasci dignatus est, pro quo hanc induta es nuditatem, pro quo has carnes expendisti, ut nihil abscondas a servo tuo, quae es, et unde, et quando, vel ob quam causam solitudinem hanc inhabitasti, sed et omnia, quae circa te sunt, edicito mihi, ut Dei magnalia facias manifesta. Sapientia enim abscondita et thesaurus occultus quae utilitas in utrisque? sicut scriptum est (Eccli. XX)? Dic mihi omnia propter Deum; nec enim pro gloriatione aut ostentatione aliquid dicis, sed ut mihi satisfacias peccatori et indigno. Credo enim Deo, cui vivis, cum quo et conversaris, quoniam ob hujuscemodi rem directus sum in hanc solitudinem, ut ea quae circa te sunt Deus faciat manifesta. Non enim nostrae virtutis est judiciis resistere Dei. Nisi fuisset acceptabile Christo Domino manifestare te et qualiter decertasti, nec teipsam permiserat videri ab aliquo, nec me confortaret tantam properare viam, nusquam valentem progredi, aut potentem de cella mea procedere.

CAP. XII.--Haec eo dicente, sed et alia plura, elevans eum mulier, dixit: Vere erubesco, ignosce, abba meus, dicere tibi turpitudinem meorum actuum; tamen quia vidisti nudum corpus meum, denudabo tibi et opera meorum actuum, ut cognoscas quam turpis luxuriae et opprobio confusionis repleta est anima mea. Non enim, ut tu ipse considerasti, propter aliquam gloriam, quae circa me sunt, volo narrare. Quid enim potero gloriari, quae diabolo vas fui electionis effecta? Scio autem quia si coepero narrare ea quae sunt de me, fugies a me, quasi quis fugiat a facie serpentis, auribus non valens audire, ob inexpedibilia quae sum operata. Dicam autem, nihil negans, sed verius referam, supplicans te prius ut non deficias orare pro me, ut misericordiam merear et inveniam in die judicii. Et senex suffusus lacrymis, flebat. Tunc coepit mulier narrare ea quae de se erant, ita dicens:

CAP. XIII.--Ego, Pater, patriam quidem Aegyptum habui: parentibus autem meis viventibus, duodecimum agens aetatis annum, affectum illorum spernens, Alexandriam veni, et quomodo quidem virginitatem meam in primis violaverim, et qualiter indesinenter et insatiabiliter vitio libidinis subjugata jacuerim, erubesco considerare. Hoc enim non breve est dicere: illud autem citius dicam, ut possis cognoscere insatiabilem vitii mei ardorem, quem habui in amorem stupri. Decem et septem et eo amplius annos transegi publice in incendio jacens luxuriae. Non propter alicujus donum virginitatem meam perdidi; neque enim ab aliquibus dare volentibus aliquid accipiebam; hoc enim libidinis furore succensa considerabam, ut amplius ad me facerem currere, gratis implens stupri mei et sceleris desiderium. Neque vero consideres quia pro divitiis nihil accipiebam; mendicans enim vivebam, aut multoties stuppam filando. Desiderium enim, ut dixi, habebam insatiabile, ita ut indesinenter me in sterquilinio luxuriae volutarem. Et hoc mihi erat placabile, et hoc vitam existimabam, si indesinenter naturae injuriam peregissem. Hoc modo me vitam ducente, vidi in quodam aestus tempore multitudinem Libyorum et

Aegyptiorum quasi ad mare concurrentem. Reperi itaque aliquem, et interrogavi: Ubi festinant viri isti, qui currunt? Dixit autem mihi: In Jerosolymam omnes ascendunt ob sanctae crucis exaltationem, quae post aliquot dies solito celebratur. Dixi autem ei et ego: Putas suscipient me, si voluero ire cum ipsis? Et ille dixit: Si habes naulum, nullus te prohibebit. Dixi ei: Vere, frater, naulum vel sumptum non habeo. Vadam autem et ascendam in unam navim, quam conduxerunt. Et licet renuant, memetipsam tradam; corpus enim meum in potestate habentes, pro naulo accipient. Propterea autem cum eis volui ambulare (abba meus, ignosce) ut multos haberem cooperatores in meae libidinis passione.

CAP. XIV.--Dixi tibi, mi domine senex, ignosce mihi, ne compellas me meam dicere confusionem. Contremisco enim, novit Dominus, maculant enim et ipsum aerem isti sermones mei. Zosimas autem terram lacrymis infundens, respondit ad eam: Dic propter Deum, o mater mea, dic, et ne praetermittas sequentia tam salutiferae narrationis. Illa autem adjungens priori narrationi, addidit haec: Ille autem adolescens audiens sermonum meorum obscuritatem, ridens discessit. Ego autem fusum, quem manu tenebam, projiciens (hunc enim post tempus conveniebat me tenere), cucurri ad mare, ubi illos perspexi currentes, et vidi juvenes aliquot in littore stantes, numero quasi decem, satis corpore vultuque acerrimos, et ad id quod mihi erat placabile, optimos. Erant autem et alii, qui jam naves ascenderant. Impudenter autem, ut mihi consuetudo erat, in medio eorum me irruenter dedi, dicens: Accipite et me vobiscum quo pergitis, non enim ero vobis implacabilis. Sed et alios sordidiores proferens sermones, omnes ad ridendum commovi. Illi autem inerubescentem motum meum videntes, accipientes me, in naviculam portaverunt. Exinde autem navigationem coepimus. Quae autem post haec acta sunt, quomodo tibi enarrare potero, o homo Dei? Quae lingua dicere potest, vel auris valet audire ea quae in navicula vel itinere facta sunt? quomodo ad peccandum et volens miseros ego compellebam nolentes. Non est narrabilis, sed inenarrabilis nequissima species, cujus tunc sum infelicibus magistra sceleribus effecta. Ergo nunc satisfactus esto, quia stupesco, quomodo meas mare illud sustinuit iniquitatum luxurias, quomodo terra non aperuit os suum, et in infernum viventem me demersit, quae tantas in laqueum mortis induxi animas. Sed, ut arbitror, meam Deus, qui neminem vult perire, sed omnes fieri salvos (I Tim. II), requirebat poenitentiam. Non enim vult mortem peccatoris, sed longanimiter exspectat, sustinens conversionem (Ezech. XVIII). Sic itaque cum magna festinatione ascendimus Jerosolymam; et quantos quidem dies ante festivitatem in civitate commorata sum, similibus nequissimis vacavi operibus, magisque pejoribus. Non enim sufficiens fui juvenibus mecum in mari luxuriantibus et in itinere, sed et alios multos peregrinos et cives in mei scelere actus congregans, coinquinavi seducens.

CAP. XV.--Quando autem venit sanctae exaltationis festivitas pretiosae crucis, ego quidem, sicut et prius, praeibam, juvenum illaqueans et capiens animas. Vidi autem primo diluculo omnes ad ecclesiam unanimiter concurrentes. Abii et ego, currens cum currentibus, et veni cum illis in atrium templi; et cum venisset hora exaltationis divinae crucis, impingebam et impingebar, repellebarque quodammodo, festinans ingredi cum populo, coarctor usque ad januam templi cum his qui ingrediebantur, cum magna laboris tribulatione appropinquans et ego infelix: quando autem ingredi volebam, illi quidem omnes sine impedimento ingrediebantur, me autem divina aliqua virtus prohibebat, non indulgens introitum. Mox igitur repulsa, ejiciebar foras; et ejecta, inveniebar sola in atrio stans. Considerans autem per muliebrem infirmitatem hoc mihi accidere, iterum aliis me immiscendo, vim mihi quodammodo faciebam introeundi, sed enim laborabam in vacuum.

CAP. XVI.--Ut enim limina vestigio contingebam, omnes interius recipiebantur, nullum habentes impedimentum, me autem solam non recipiebat; sed quasi militaris multitudo esset taxata ut mihi ingredienti aditum clauderet, ita me repentina aliqua prohibebat virtus, et iterum inveniebar in atrio. Hoc ter et quater passa et facere conans, nihilque proficiens, desperans de caetero, et amplius nusquam progredi valens (factum quippe fuerat corpus meum a vi comprimentium valde confractum), recedens discessi, et steti in quodam angulo atrii templi; et vix aliquando, ob quam causam prohibebar videre vivificum lignum in cogitationem reduxi. Tetigit enim mentem et cordis mei oculos intellectus salutis, recogitans quia squalida actuum meorum scelera mihi introeundi aditum obserabant. Coepi itaque flens nimium conturbari et pectus tundere, atque suspiria de profundo cordis proferens, et gemens ejulansque prospexi in loco in quo stabam, sursum imaginem sanctae Dei genitricis stantem, et aio, ad eam intendens et indeclinanter attendens; Domina virgo, quae Deum genuisti secundum carnem, scio quia nec condecens nec opportunum sit me sic horridam adorare imaginem tuam vel contemplari oculis tantis sordibus pollutis, quae esse virgo dignosceris et casta, quae corpus et animam habes immaculatam: justum est me luxuriosam a tua purissima castitatis munditia abominari et projici. Tamen quoniam, ut audivi, ob hoc effectus est Deus homo, quem ipsa digna genuisti, ut peccatores vocaret ad poenitentiam, adjuva me solitariam et nullum habentem adjutorium, percipe confessionem meam, et mihi licentiam tribue ecclesiae patefactum ingredi aditum, et non efficiar aliena a visione pretiosissimi ligni, in quo affixus Deus homo, quem concipiens ipsa virgo peperisti, et proprium sanguinem dedit pro mea liberatione. Jube, o Domina, et mihi indignae ob divinae crucis salutationem januam patefieri, et te ex te genito Christo dignissimam do fidejussorem, quia nunquam ultra meam carnem coinquinabo per horrida immistionum ludibria; sed mox ut filii tui, Virgo sancta, videro lignum, saeculo et actibus ejus, et omnibus quae in eo sunt renuntio, et continuo egredior ubicunque ipsa ut fidejussor me duxeris.

CAP. XVII.--Haec dicens, et quasi aliquam satisfactionem recipiens, fidei succensa calore, et de pietatis visceribus Dei genitricis praesumens, movi me de eodem loco, in quo stans feci orationem; et veniens, iterum ingredientibus me miscui, et ultra non erat qui me repelleret, neque qui me prohiberet appropinquare januis, quibus in templum introibant. Accepit ergo me tremor validus et extasis, et tota ex omnibus tremebunda turbabar. Itaque conjungens me ad januam, cujus mihi aditus primo claudebatur (quasi omnis virtus quae prius ingredi me prohibebat, post autem viam ingrediendi pararet), ita absque impedimenti labore introivi, et sic intra sancta sanctorum reperta sum, et pretiosi ac vivifici crucis ligni adorare mysterium digna habita sum: et tunc vidi Dei sacramenta, et qualiter est paratus suscipere poenitentes. Tunc projiciens me coram in terram, et sanctum illud exosculans pavimentum, exibam. Currens autem ad illam quae me fidedixit, veni restans. Conjunxi igitur me in illum locum ubi fidedictionis conscriptum erat chirographum, et genu curvans coram vultu sanctae Virginis Dei genitricis, his imprecata sum verbis: Tu quidem semper, o benignissima Domina, tuam ostendisti pietatis misericordiam: tu non indignam supplicationem projecisti; vidi gloriam quam peccatores merito non videmus, gloriam omnipotentis Dei qui per te suscipit peccatorum poenitentiam. Quid amplius peccatrix et misera valeo recordari aut enarrare? Tempus est jam implere quae fidedixi, fide dilectionis tuae placita. Nunc ubi tibi complacet, dirige me. Esto mihi salutis ducatrix, et veritatis magistra, praecedens me in viam quae ducit ad poenitentiam. Et haec dicens, audivi vocem alicujus a longe clamantis: Jordanem si transieris, bonam invenies requiem. Ego autem hanc vocem audiens, et pro me factam credens, lacrymans exclamavi, et ad Dei genitricis imaginem prospiciens vociferavi: Domina, Domina, Regina totius orbis, per quam humano generi salus advenit, noli me derelinquere. Et haec dicens, de atrio templi sum egressa, et festinanter ambulabam. Exeunte autem me, vidit me quis, et dedit mihi tres nummos, dicens: Accipe haec, nonna: ego autem accipiens, tres ex eis panes comparavi, et hos accepi benedictioni mei itineris congruos. Interrogavi eum qui panes vendebat: Unde et qualis via esse noscitur, homo, quae ducit ad Jordanem? Et cognoscens portam civitatis quae in illa latera pergit, currens iter agebam plorans.

CAP. XVIII.--Interrogationi autem interrogationem annectens, reliquum diei consumpsi iter properans: erat autem hora diei tertia, quando pretiosam et sanctam crucem videre merui. Et sole jam ad occasum declinante, ecclesiam beati Joannis Baptistae positam juxta Jordanem conspexi, et in eodem templo ingressa adorans continuo in Jordanem descendi, et ex illa sancta aqua manus et faciem lavi. Communicavi autem vivifica et intemerata Christi Domini sacramenta, in eadem sancta praecursoris et Baptistae Joannis basilica, et tunc unius panis medietatem comedi, et ex aqua Jordanis bibi, in terra nocte quiescens. Lucescente in crastino in partem aliam transivi, et iterum petii ductricem meam ut me dirigeret ubi ei placitum esset. Deveni autem in hanc solitudinem, et ex tunc usque hodie elongavi fugiens, exspectans Deum meum, qui salvos facit pusillos et magnos, qui convertuntur ad eum (Ps. LIV). Zosimas dixit ad eam: Quot anni sunt, o domina, ex quo hanc inhabitas solitudinem? Respondit mulier: Quadraginta septem anni sunt, ut considero, ex quo de sancta civitate egressa sum. Dixit autem Zosimas: Et quid invenire ad esum potuisti, o mi, aut invenis, Domina. Respondit mulier: Duos semis quidem panes Jordanem transmeavi deportans; et qui post modicum arefacti quasi lapides obduruerunt, et modicum quid usque ad aliquos annos comedens transegi. Dixit autem Zosimas: Et sic absque dolore transisti tanti temporis longitudinem? nihil repentinae immutationis et conturbationis sensisti calorem? Illa dixit: Rem nunc me interrogas, quam dicens valde contremisco, si ad commemorationem venero tantorum quae sustinui periculorum, et cogitationum quae inique perturbaverunt me: timeo enim ne ab eisdem aliquam patiar tribulationem. Dixit Zosimas: Nihil relinquas, o domina, quae non indices. Semel enim in hoc te manifestam cognovimus ordine, omnia te indiminute oportet nos edocere.

CAP. XIX.--Illa autem dixit ei: Crede, abba, decem et septem annis feris immansuetis et irrationalibus eluctans desideriis, dum cibum initiabam, desiderio mihi erant carnes; concupiebam pisces quos Aegyptus habebat; desiderabam etiam vinum delectabile mihi; multum enim delectabar in vino, et superabundantius usque ad ebrietatem bibebam, et nunc mihi erat valde in desiderio, eo quod multum uterer, dum essem in saeculo. Hic autem aquam omnino non habens, vehementissime urebar, et sustinebam necessitatis periculum. Fiebat mihi et de luxuriosis canticis nimium desiderium, perturbans et reducens ad memoriam daemoniorum cantica decantare, quae in saeculo dediceram. Mox autem lacrymans, et pectus meum percutiens, meipsam ad memoriam reducebam de convenienti fidedictionis quam feceram, egrediens contra hanc solitudinem. Veniebam autem per cognitionem ante imaginem sanctae Dei genitricis, quae me et in fide sua suscepit, et ante illam plorabam, ut effugaret a me cogitationes quae miserrimam meam animam affligebant. Quando autem superflue dolenterque lacrymabar, et viriliter pectus meum tundebam, tunc videbam lumen undique circumfulgens me, et serenitas mihi quaedam stabilis mox fiebat. Cogitationes autem quae ad fornicationem iterum compellebant me, quomodo tibi enarrare possum? Abba, ignosce. Ignis intus infelix corpus meum nimis succendebat, et totam me per omnia exurebat, et ad desiderium commissionis pertrahebat. Dum ergo mihi talis ascenderet cogitatio, prosternebam meipsam in terram, et lacrymis terram infundens, ipsam mihi veraciter astare sperans, quae me fidedixerat, minanti me compellatione exaggerare furentem, quasi praevaricanti, et poenas praevaricationis mihi imminentes ira mucronis contra me agentem. Non enim ante surgebam de terra, nisi prius illa dulcissima lux illuminaret me solito, et cogitationes me perturbantes effugaret. Semper itaque cordis mei oculos ad illam fidejussorem meam sine cessatione erigebam, deprecans eam auxiliari mihi in hac solitudine et poenitentia. Habui ergo adjutricem et coadjutricem ipsam, quae genuit castitatis auctorem, et sic decem et septem annorum curriculis cum multis, ut dixi, usque hodie periculis eluctata sum. A tunc ergo adjutorium meum Dei genitrix astitit mihi, per omnia in omnibus me dirigens. Dixit autem Zosimas: Non habuisti cibum aut vestimentum? Et illa dixit: Panes quidem illos, sicut jam dixi, decem et septem expendens annis, deinde nutriebar herbis quae inveniebantur per solitudinem. Indumentum autem quod habui, transmeato Jordane nimia vetustate scissum et consumptum est. Multam ergo glaciali frigore et aestus ardore necessitatem sustinui, concremata aestus incenato, et nimio trigoris tempore gelu rigescens et tremens, multoties in terram cadens absque spiritu jacebam immobilis, multis et diversis necessitatibus et tentationibus immensis eluctans, per omnia usque in hanc diem virtus Dei multis modis miseram animam meam et corpus meum custodivit. Recordans enim de qualibus malis liberavit me Dominus, esca nutrior inconsummabili, et satietatis possideo epulas spem salutis meae. Nutrior autem et cooperior tegmine verbi Dei, qui continet omnia (Deut. VIII). Non enim in solo pane vivit homo (Matt. III), et non habentes operimentum petrae circumdati sunt tegmine hi qui se peccati exspoliaverunt tunica (Job XXIV, juxta LXX).

CAP. XX.--Audiens autem Zosimas quoniam Scripturarum testimonia proferebat ex libris Moysi videlicet et beati Job sive Psalmorum, dixit ad eam: Psalmos, o mater, didicisti, vel alios libros sacrae Scripturae legisti? Illa autem hoc audiens, subridens dixit ad eum: Crede mihi, non vidi hominem ex quo Jordanem transivi, nisi te hodie: sed neque feram aut aliud animal qualecunque, ex quo in hanc deveni solitudinem. Litteras autem nunquam alicubi didici, sed neque psallentem aut legentem aliquem auscultavi. Sermo autem Dei vivus et efficax intellectum intrinsecus docet humanum. (Heb. IV). Huc usque finis eorum quae mea sunt. Nunc autem obsecrans quaeso te per incarnationem Verbi Dei ut ores pro me luxuriosa. Et cum haec dixisset, cucurrit senex et genu flexo se in terram prosternere, vociferans et dicens: Benedictus Dominus Deus qui facit mirabilia magna solus, gloriosa et vehementer stupenda quibus non est numerus (Job IX). Benedictus es, Domine Deus, qui ostendisti mihi quanta largiris timentibus te. Vere enim non derelinquis quaerentes te, Domine (Psal. IX). Illa autem apprehendens senem, non permisit in terram perfecte prosterni, sed dixit ei: Haec quae audisti, homo, obtestor te per Dominum Salvatorem nostrum Jesum Christum, nemini dixeris, quoadusque Deus de vinculo carnis absolvat me. His omnibus acceptis in pace, et iterum hoc eodem tempore adveniente anno apparebo tibi, et videbis me, Dei nos gubernante gratia. Fac autem propter Dominum, quod nunc tibi injungo, ut sacris jejuniis recurrentibus anni venturi non transeas Jordanem, ut consuetudinem habetis in monasterio. Stupebat autem Zosimas, audiens quoniam et canonem monasterii inscia quasi quae nosset dicebat; nihilque aliud clamabat nisi gloriam Dei, qui majora quam petitur diligentibus se largitur. Illa autem dixit: Sustine ut dixi, abba, in monasterio; neque etsi exire volueris quoquam, valebis. Vespere autem sacratissimo Dominicae coenae, divini corporis et vivifici sanguinis portionem in vase sacro dignoque tanti mysterii affer, et sustine me in parte Jordanis quae conjungitur saeculo, et veniens vivifica accipiam dona. Ex quo enim in ecclesia beatissimi Praecursoris, priusquam transirem Jordanem, communicavi, deinceps usque nunc nunquam communicavi, nunquam usque nunc sanctificationis hujus usa sum portione; et ideo, deprecor, meam ne spernas petitionem, sed per omnia ipsa vivifica atque divina mysteria affer in ea hora, qua Dominus discipulos divinae coenae participes fecit. Joanni autem abbati monasterii, in quo habitas, edicito: Attende tibi ipsi et gregi tuo; aliqua enim fiunt ibi emendatione indigentia. Sed nolo te haec nunc ei dicere, sed quando tibi praeceperit Deus. Haec dicens, orationem a sene postulando, in interiorem solitudinem velocius festinavit.

CAP. XXI.--Zosimas autem prosternens se, osculabatur terrae locum, in quo ejus vestigia steterant, dans gloriam Deo: immensasque gratias agens, reversus est, laudans et benedicens Dominum Deum nostrum Jesum Christum. Iterum autem remeans ejusdem solitudinis iter, quo venerat, conjunxit in monasterio eo tempore, quo consueverant ii qui in eodem morabantur. Et totum quidem annum illum tacuit, minime audens quidpiam dicere ex his quae viderat; in seipso autem deprecabatur Deum, ut iterum ei ostenderet desiderabilem vultum. Suspirabat autem, annui cursus considerans tarditatem. Quando autem advenit sacra jejuniorum initiata prima Dominica, mox post solitam orationem alii quidem psallentes exierunt: ipse autem modica febris infirmitate detentus, mansit intus in monasterio. Recordatus est autem Zosimas sibi praedictum sanctae illius, quia neque volens exire valebis. Aliquantis autem elapsis diebus, ab infirmitate sublevatus, in monasterio conversabatur. Quando reversi sunt monachi sacratae coenae vespere, fecit quod ei jussum est: et mittens in modico calice intemerati corporis portionem et pretiosi sanguinis Domini nostri Jesu Christi, posuit in canistro carycas paucas et palmarum fructus, id est dactylos, et parum lenticulae infusae in aquis; et venit tarde, et ad ripam Jordanis sedebat, adventum sanctae praestolans. Beatissima autem illa tardante muliere, Zosimas non dormitavit, sed sollicite attendebat solitudinem, sustinens quod videre desiderabat. Dicebat autem in semetipso: Nunquid veniens, dum me non invenit, reversa est? Haec dicens, flebat; et elevans in coelum oculos, suppliciter Deum deprecabatur, dicens: Non me alienes, Domine, iterum videre, quam me videre tribuisti. Non vadam vacuus, peccata mea portans in increpatione.

CAP. XXII.--Haec orans cum lacrymis, alia in eum cogitatio incidit. Quid itaque si venerit, faciet? quomodo transiet Jordanem, quia navicula non est? qualiter ad me indignum perveniet? Heu me infelicem! heu quis me tam justae speciei alienavit? Haec sene cogitante, ecce sancta illa advenit, et in parte alia fluminis stetit, unde venerat. Zosimas autem videns eam, surrexit gaudens, et exsultans nimis glorificabat Deum. Lucta autem certaminis in ejus fluctuabat cogitationis intentione, quia non potest Jordanis transire fluenta. Et respiciens senex, vidit eam vexillo crucis aquas Jordanis signantem. Totius enim tunc noctis tenebras splendor illuminabat lunae, quia tempus recursus illius erat. Statim autem ut signum crucis impressit, ascendit super aquas; et ambulans super liquidum aequoris fluctum, veniebat quasi per solidum iter. Zosimas autem stupens, et genua flectere nitens, clamans desuper aquas prohibuit, dicens: Quid facis, abba, quia et sacerdos Dei es, et divina portas mysteria? Qui statim obedivit dicenti. Illa autem descendens de aquis, dixit seni: Benedic, Pater, benedic. Ille autem cum magna festinatione respondit (stupor enim nimius invaserat eum in tam glorioso miraculo), et dixit: Vere non mentitur Deus, qui pollicitus est sibi similes esse eos qui semetipsos purificant. Gloria tibi, Christe Deus noster, qui ostendisti mihi per ancillam tuam hanc, quantum mea consideratione inferior sum mensura verae perfectionis. Haec eo dicente, postulavit mulier ut sanctum diceret Symbolum, et sic Dominicam inchoaret orationem. Et expleto Pater noster, sancta, sicut mos est, pacis osculum obtulit seniori; et sic vivifica mysteriorum suscipiens dona, in coelum extensis manibus ingemiscens cum lacrymis, ita clamabat: Nunc dimittis, Domine, ancillam tuam secundum verbum tuum in pace; quia viderunt oculi mei salutare tuum (Luc. II). Et seni dixit: Ignosce, abba, et aliud meae petitionis imple mandatum. Vade nunc ad monasterium, Dei pace gubernatus; recursu autem anni advenientis iterum veni in illo torrente, in quo tecum sum prius locuta. Per omnia non omittas, sed propter Deum veni: et videbis me iterum, qualiter Deus voluerit. Ille autem respondit ad eam: Utinam esset possibile nunc tua sequi vestigia, et sui pretiosissimi vultus visione frui! Oro, mater, ut unam senis petitiunculam facias, et modicum cibi ex eo quod huc attuli, digneris accipere. Et haec dicens, ostendit ei quod secum detulerat canistrum. Illa autem extremis digitis lenticulam contigit, et tria tollens grana proprio intulit ori, sufficere dicens gratiam Spiritus, ut custodiret animae substantiam immaculatam. Tunc dicit seni: Ora pro me propter Deum, et meae memor esto semper infelicitatis. Ille pedes ejus sanctos contingens, cum lacrymis deprecabatur, ut oraret pro Ecclesia, et pro imperio, et pro se, et sic dimisit eam abire flens et ejulans. Non enim audebat eam multum detinere, quae nec, si vellet, poterat detineri.

CAP. XXIII.--Illa autem crucis iterum impressione Jordanem signans, ascendit ambulans super liquidum elementum, et transivit sicut ante veniens fecerat. Senex autem reversus est gaudio et tremore repletus. Et semetipsum reprehendebat, poenitens, quia nomen sanctae ut cognosceret, non inquisivit; sperabat tamen advenienti hoc consequi anno.

CAP. XXIV.--Transacto autem eodem anni cursu, venit iterum in vastam deserti solitudinem, expletis omnibus secundum consuetudinem, festinabat ad gloriosam illam visionem intuendam. Perambulans autem solitudinem, et non inveniens aliqua cupiti loci indicantia signa, dextra laevaque aspiciens, intuitum oculorum deducens, et lustrans ubique sicut citissimus venator, sicubi suavissimam comprehenderet feram. Ut autem nihil ullo modo vidit quoquam moventem, coepit seipsum lugens infundere lacrymis. Tunc elevans oculos, orabat dicens: Obsecro mihi ostende, Domine, in corpore angelum, cui totus comparari indignus est mundus.

CAP. XXV.--Haec orando, pervenit ad locum, qui in similitudine fuerat designatus torrentis, et in extrema ejus parte superiore vidit splendentem solem; et aspiciens, vidit sanctae mortuum jacens corpus, et manus, ut oportet, sic compositas, et ad Orientem jacens corpus aspiciens. Currens autem, lacrymis lavit beatissimae pedes, non enim aliud corporis membrum audebat contingere. Lacrymans autem aliquandiu, et psalmos dicens tempori et rei congruentes, fecit sepulturae orationem, et dicebat sibi ipsi: Forsitan non complacet sanctae haec fieri. Haec eo cogitante, designata scriptura erat in terra, ubi hoc legebatur: «Sepeli, abba Zosima, miserae Mariae corpusculum. Redde terrae, quod suum est, et pulveri adjice pulverem. Ora tantum pro me propter Dominum transeunte mense Parmothi secundum Aegyptios; qui est secundum Romanos Aprilis die nona, id est, V Idus Aprilis salutiferae passionis, post divinae et sacrae coenae communionem.»

CAP. XXVI.--Has senex cum legisset litteras, cogitabat quidem prius quisnam esset qui scripsit: illa enim, ut dixerat, litteras ignorabat. In hoc tamen valde exsultans gaudebat, quia ejus sanctum didicit nomen. Cogitavit vero quia mox ut divina in Jordane mysteria participavit, in eadem hora in locum illum venit, ubi mox de hoc mundo transivit, et idem iter, quod Zosimas per dies viginti ambulans vix consummavit laborans, unius horae cursu Maria consumpsit, et statim migravit ad Dominum. Glorificans autem Zozimas Dominum, et lacrymis corpus ejus infundens: Tempus est, inquit, miser Zosima, quod tuum est, perfice. Sed quid faciam infelix, quia unde fodore valeam, non habeo? Deest sarculum, non est rastrum, nihilque ex omnibus habeo prae manibus. Haec illo in corde suo dicente, vidit parvum lignum et modicum jacere: quod assumens, coepit fodere. Valde autem durior erat terra, et multum fortissima, et nequaquam valebat fodere, quia et jejunio confectus, et longi itineris fatigatione nimis erat defectus. Laborabat enim, et suspiriis nimiis urgebatur, et sudoribus madefactus, ingemuit graviter ex ipso cordis sui profundo. Et respiciens, vidit ingentis formae leonem juxta corpus sanctae stantem, et ejus plantas lambentem. Videns autem, contremunt praepavore grandissimae ferae illius, praecipue quia audierat sanctam feminam illam dicentem quia nunquam aliquam feram viderat. Signo autem se crucis confirmavit undique credens quia illaesum custodire valet eum virtus jacentis. Leo autem coepit innuere seni, blandis eum nutibus salutans. Zozimas autem dixit leoni: Quoniam a Deo missus venisti, maxime ferarum, ut hujus Dei famulae corpus terrae commendetur, exple opus officii, ut possit sepeliri ejus corpusculum. Ego enim senectute confectus non valeo fodere, sed nec congruum quid habeo ad hoc opus exercendum; et iterum tanti itineris longitudine properare non valeo ut afferam. Tu divino jussu hoc opus cum ungulis facito, ut commendemus terrae hoc sanctum corpusculum.

CAP. XXVII.--Continuo autem, juxta senis sermonem, leo cum brachiis fecit ipse foveam, quanta ad sepeliendum sanctae corpusculum sufficere posset. Senex vero lacrymis pedes sanctae abluens, et multipliciter effusa prece exorans pro omnibus eam tunc et amplius pro se exorare, operuit terra corpusculum nudum, astante leone, sicut eam prius repererat, et nihil aliud habens, nisi illud scissum vestimentum, quod ei jam ante projecerat Zozimas, ex quo Maria quaedam sui corporis texit membra. Deinde recedunt pariter; et leo quidem in interiora solitudinis quasi ovis mansueta abscessit; Zozimas autem reversus est, benedicens et laudans Deum, et hymnum laudis decantans Christo Domino nostro. Veniens autem in coenobio, omnia eis ab initio retulit, et nihil abscondit ex omnibus quae vidit et audivit, ut omnes audientes magnalia Dei, nimio stupore admirarentur, et cum timore et amore magna fide celebrarent beatissimae sanctae transitus diem. Joannes autem abbas invenit quosdam indigentes emendari, juxta sanctae illius sermonem, et hos, miserante Domino Deo, convertit. Zozimas autem in eodem degens monasterio, implevit annos centum, et tunc migravit ad Dominum in pace, gratia Domini nostri Jesu Christi, cui cum Patre gloria et honor et imperium una cum sancto vivificatore et adorando Spiritu, nunc et semper et in saecula saeculorum. Amen.

The Scriptorium Project is the work of a small group of lay people of various apostolic churches who are interested in the preservation, transmission, and translation of the works of the early and medieval church. Our efforts are to make the works of the church fathers accessible to anyone who might have an interest in Christian antiquities and the theological, philosophical, and moral writings that have become the bedrock of Western Civilization.

To-date, our releases have pulled from the Greek, Syriac, Georgian, Latin, Celtic, Ethiopian, and Coptic traditions of Christianity, and have been pulled from sundry local traditions and languages.

Other Titles and Translations by D.P. Curtin:

Lebor Gabala Erenn by Nennius the Monk (2017)
The Eight Vices by Eutropis of Valencia (2017)
Three Letters from the Companion of the Bulgars by St. Rupert of Juvavum (2017)
Privileges of the Abbot of Canterbury by St. Augustine of Canterbury (2017)
Chapters on Church Law by Pope Adrian I (2017)
A Song of Aethelwolf by Aethelwolf of Lindisfarne (2017)
Humility & Obedience by Novatus the Catholic (2017)
Nicene Canons in the Old Nubian Language (2018)
Apology to Gunthamund, King of Vandals by Aemeilius Dracontius (2018)
Fragments by St. Ephraim of Antioch (2018)
An Account of the Gallican Liturgy by St. Germain of Paris (2018)
Visigothic Chronicle by John of Biclaro (2018)
Preludes by Photius of Paris (2018)
First Book of Ethiopian Maccabees (2018)
Chronicon: a short chronicle of Visigothic Spain by Eutrandus of Ticino (2019)
Decrees of Aethelbert by St. Aethelbert, King of Kent (2019)
The Measure to be taxed for Penance by St. Columba of Iona (2019)
The Privileges of Rome by Louis I the Pious (2019)
Protoevangelium of James: Greek and English Texts (2019)
Edicts of the Synod of Paris by Chlothar II, King of Franks (2019)
The Synod of Rome by St. Boniface IV of Rome (2019)
Letter to Pope Theodore by Victor of Carthage (2020)
The Decree of 610 by Gundemar, King of Visigoths (2020)
Laws of the Church by Chlothar III, King of Franks (2020)
Donations by St. Aethelbert, King of Kent (2020)
The Mystical Interpretation by St. Aileran the Wise (2020)
Laws of the Church by St. Dagobert II, King of Franks (2020)
The Old Nubian Miracle of St. Mena (2021)
Council of Seleucia-Ctesiphon by Mar Isaac of Seleucia (2021)
A Book of Placesnames from 'Acts' by St. Jerome (2021)
About Fifteen Problems by St. Albertus Magnus (2022)
Testament of Some Former Things by John Scotus Eriugena (2022)
The Georgian Synaxarium (2022)
Instructions: Counsel for Novices by St. Ammonas the Hermit (2022)
The Syriac Menologium and Martyrology (2022)
Book on Religious Exercise and Quiet by St. Isaiah the Solitary (2022)
Vision of Theophilus by St. Cyril of Alexandria (2022)
On Fate (De Fato) by St. Albertus Magnus (2023)
Fragments of 'Chronicle' by Hippolytus of Thebes (2023)
Life of the Blessed Theotokos by Epiphanius Monachus (2023)
Syriac Life of John the Baptist by Serapion the Presbyter (2023)